Lion Bible Favourites

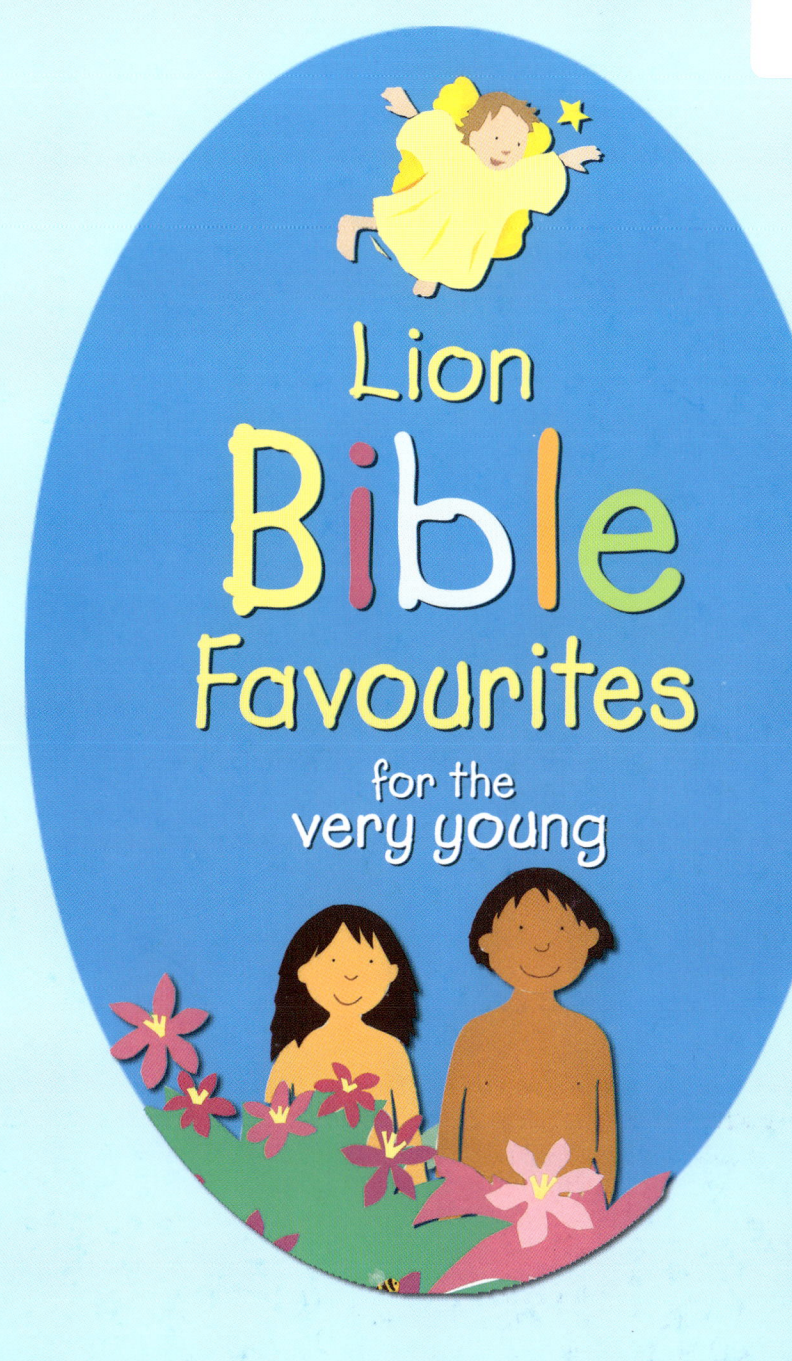

for the very young

LION CHILDREN'S

Contents

6 In the Beginning
by Lois Rock
illustrated by Alex Ayliffe

10 The First Rainbow
by Su Box
illustrated by Susie Poole

16 Baby Moses, Brave Moses
by Lois Rock
illustrated by Richard Johnson

20 David and His Song
by Lois Rock
illustrated by Ruth Rivers

24 Jonah and the Big Fish
by Sarah Toulmin
illustrated by Kristina Stephenson

30 Daniel and the Lions
by Sophie Piper
illustrated by Estelle Corke

34 Little Baby Jesus
by Lois Rock
illustrated by Carolyn Cox

38 Jesus and the Children
by Sophie Piper
illustrated by Dubravka Kolanovic

40 Looking High and Low for One Lost Sheep
by Christina Goodings
illustrated by Alex Ayliffe

44 The Story of the Good Samaritan
by Lois Rock
illustrated by Anthony Lewis

48 The Great Feast
by Lois Rock
illustrated by Gail Newey

52 The Loving Father
by Pat Alexander
illustrated by Leon Baxter

56 The Cross
by Mary Joslin
illustrated by Angelo Ruta

58 The Easter Angels
by Mary Joslin
illustrated by Elena Temporin

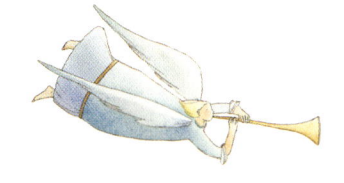

In the Beginning

by Lois Rock
illustrated by Alex Ayliffe

In the beginning, there was nothing but dark.

Then God spoke: 'Let there be light.'

And the very first light shone brightly.

God spread the sky wide above the ocean and God folded the land to make hills and valleys.

God covered the earth with plants: grasses and flowers, vegetables and trees.

The sun shone in the daytime, and the moon and stars waited for their turn in the night-time.

God made all the creatures.

Birds flew in the sky.

Fish swam in the seas.

Animals leaped and ran and scurried and hurried all over the land. They made themselves homes in holes and burrows and nests and dens.

Then God made people – man and woman.

'Welcome,' said God. 'You are my friends, and I want you to be safe and happy. Take care of the good world I have made for you.

'Never choose to know about bad things: they will only make you sad.'

Everything was perfect.

The world was a paradise garden until the snake came and whispered:

'Go on: find out about bad things as well as good things. Then you will be as wise as God. All you have to do is eat this fruit… the one God told you not to eat.'

All at once, the world changed.

The man and the woman were no longer friends with God.

Instead, they felt all alone in an unkind world. They had to work very hard for everything they needed.

'Can things ever be put right again?' they wondered. People have been wondering ever since.

The First Rainbow

by Su Box
illustrated by Susie Poole

Long ago, the people on earth were being bad. This made God very sad. He wanted to wash his world clean again. He would make it rain.
But there was one good man. His name was Noah.
'Build a boat,' God said to Noah. 'A boat to float when it rains, for water will flood the earth.'
So Noah did.

'Fill the boat with animals. Two of every kind,' God said to Noah.

So Noah did.

There were all kinds of birds and animals:

BIG and small...

FIERCE and friendly...

FURRY and smooth...

NOISY and *quiet*.

At last all the animals were on board. There was just enough room for Noah and his family too.

Then God shut the door of the boat.

It began to rain. It rained for forty days. It rained for forty nights.

Down, down, down fell the rain.

Up, up, up rose the water.

Soon the boat was afloat. Noah could see nothing but water everywhere.

At long, long last it stopped raining.

Days passed.

Weeks passed.

Months passed.

But still there was water everywhere.

The birds and animals were bored.

They trum**pet**ed...
   and *grunted*...
   and b l e a t e d ...
   and *brayed*.

At long, long last the boat stopped on a mountain top. The water was going down!

Noah let a raven fly from the boat. It did not come back.

Then Noah let a dove fly from the boat. It came back with a leaf in its beak. Plants were growing. The land was dry!

The birds and animals wanted to go outside.
They **chattered**...
and c h e e p e d ...
and CAWED and *ROARED*.

'Come out!' God said to Noah. 'The world is clean again. Now you and your family and all the animals must fill it with new life.'

So the birds and animals left the boat:
creeping and *crawling*...
running and j^{u}mp^{i}ng...
soaring and diving...
s l i t h e r i n g and *shuffling*.

'Thank you, God,' said Noah, 'for keeping us safe.'

Then God painted the world's first rainbow as a promise that he would never send a flood like that again. He was happy with his clean, new world.

Baby Moses, Brave Moses

by Lois Rock
illustrated by Richard Johnson

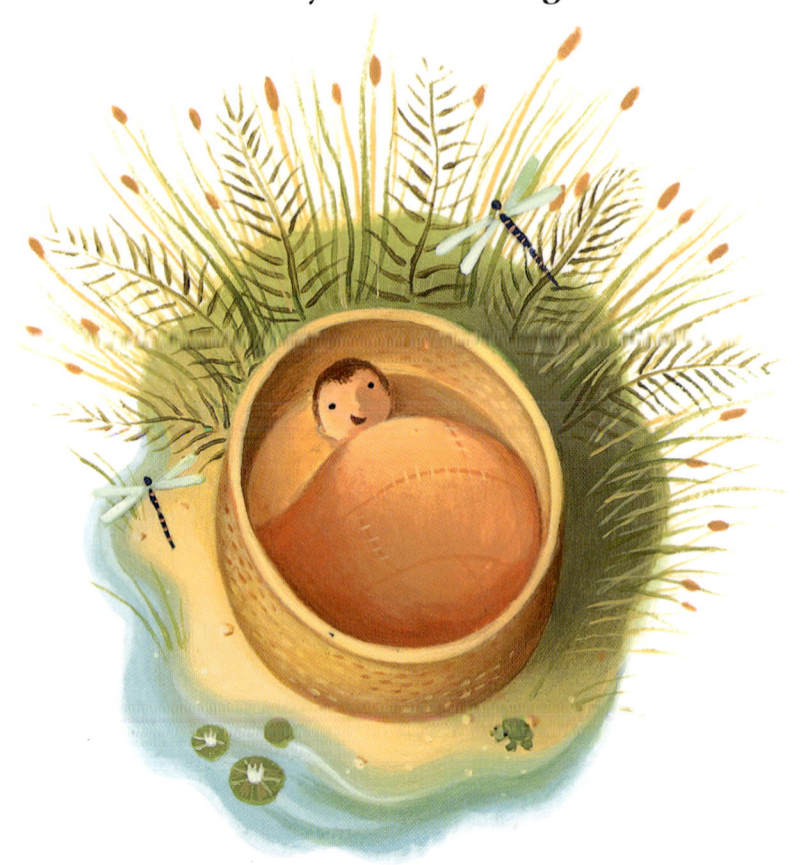

Baby Moses, in his cradle, down by the river;
safe in his cradle where the reeds grow tall –
he didn't know about the king, he hadn't heard of soldiers,
he didn't know of anything to worry him at all.

Down by the river where the wind sighs and whispers
the king's lovely daughter came to bathe in the pool.
'Go,' she told her servant, 'I can see something floating –
there, by the river, where the reeds grow tall.'

They went and fetched the cradle and baby safely
   sleeping,
he opened his eyes, but he didn't cry or whine.
'Poor little baby!' said the king's lovely daughter,
'I'm going to keep him safe, I'm going to make him mine.'

Brave man Moses led his people to the shoreline –

down to the shoreline where the reeds grow tall.

They knew about the king, and they could hear the sound
  of horses,

for soldiers in their chariots had come to take them all.

Down by the shoreline where the wind sighs and whispers,
brave man Moses held his arms up high,
and God made the wind blow a path right through the water
and Moses led the people through and kept them safe and dry.

David and His Song

by Lois Rock

illustrated by Ruth Rivers

Long ago, in the hilltop town of Bethlehem, lived a boy named David.

He was the youngest in his family, and his job was to look after the sheep.

Out on the hillsides, he discovered the places where the grass grew lush and green.

Down in the valleys, he found where the water ran clean and clear.

While the sheep were grazing, David had plenty of time to sit and think.

As he sat, he practised throwing stones from his sling. He needed to be able to scare away wild animals.

He made himself a harp from wood and string and

practised playing. He made up his own tunes and sang along.

Everyone who passed by smiled when they heard David sing, for his voice was clear and sweet and strong.

One day, David went to visit his older brothers. They were soldiers in King Saul's army, and there was bad news.

'The enemy have a champion called Goliath,' the soldiers said. 'He is a giant and he has the very best weapons. If anyone can beat him, we win the war. If not, the enemy will treat us cruelly.'

'I shall fight Goliath,' declared David boldly. 'I dare because God will help me.'

He didn't take any armour. He didn't even take a sword. David fought as he fought against the animals: he beat Goliath with a stone from his sling.

King Saul was very pleased with David and made him a musician at the royal court.

David also became a very fine soldier. He faced many dangers and won many victories.

So many people admired him that, after Saul died, David became the new king.

He was rich. He was powerful. Safe in his new palace, he had time to sit and think.

He had a harp made from the finest polished wood and the smoothest, strongest strings. He made up his own tunes and sang along.

He made up a new song: about how God had always looked after him when he was a shepherd boy and when he was a soldier.

*Dear God, you are my shepherd,
you give me all I need,
you take me where the grass grows green
and I can safely feed.*

*You take me where the water
is quiet and cool and clear;
and there I rest and know I'm safe
for you are always near.*

*You save me from my enemies
and they can plainly see
the special loving kindness that
you always show to me.*

Jonah and the Big Fish

by Sarah Toulmin
illustrated by Kristina Stephenson

Once there was a man named Jonah.

He was the kind of person who listens to God, and one day God gave him a special message.

'Please go to Nineveh, Jonah. The people there do bad things. You must tell them to stop.'

Jonah sulked.

'Hmphh. I don't like the people in Nineveh. I don't want to go there,' he said to himself.

'In fact, I'll go somewhere else.'

Jonah went to a town by the sea.

'Where is that boat going?' asked Jonah.

'Spain,' replied the sailor.

'I want to go there,' said Jonah.

'Come aboard,' replied the sailor.

The boat set out across the sea. Night came and the sky went dark.

Then God sent a storm; a fierce storm, a wild storm, a storm that made the waves go

CRASH!

A storm that made the wind roar *RAAAH!*

The boat rocked – up and down, up and down, up and down.

'Help!' shouted the sailors. 'We're all going to sink into the sea!'

'Oh dear,' sobbed Jonah. 'It's all my fault. I disobeyed God, and God has sent the storm to punish me. You must throw me off the boat before everything goes wrong.'

'You?' gasped the sailors. 'You have done something to make God send a storm?

'Well, we'd like to take you to shore but sadly it's

SPLISH!

Jonah sank into the
**deep
deep
sea.**
A big fish came by,
opened its mouth and...

GULP!

'Oh no!' moaned Jonah. 'I'll never see the places I love again! Dear God, only you can help me now!' All at once, then, to his great surprise there came an enormous...

Hiccup!

'Oh,' said Jonah. 'I'm safe. On land.

'Whatever shall I do? I know! I'll go to Nineveh. I'll tell the people to stop doing bad things.'

The people of Nineveh listened to Jonah.

'Oh dear!' they said. 'We have been bad.'

'We're very sorry, God,' they cried. 'Please forgive us.'

Jonah went off and sulked. 'I wanted God to punish them,' he muttered. 'Now God is going to listen to their weeping and wailing. And then he'll change his mind.'

Jonah stomped away from Nineveh.

He made a little house to shelter him from the sun. A plant grew next to it.

'This is better,' said Jonah. 'At least I've got a nice place in the shade.'

In the night, a worm nibbled the plant. It drooped and died.

'My plant!' wailed Jonah. 'My poor, poor plant.'

'Are you sad about a plant?' asked God. 'Well, I want you to understand something. You loved a plant that grew by itself.

'I love the people of Nineveh and all their animals too.'

Daniel and the Lions

by Sophie Piper
illustrated by Estelle Corke

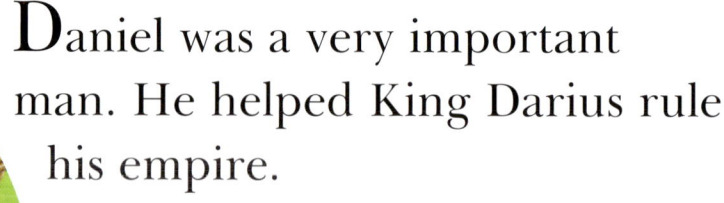

Daniel was a very important man. He helped King Darius rule his empire.

He worked hard, and he was very good at his job.

'I think I shall put Daniel in charge of the empire,' said Darius.

The other people who worked for Darius were very cross.

'Why is Daniel getting a better job?' they muttered. 'How we wish we could get rid of him.'

'We need a secret plan,' said one. 'Listen.'

They huddled close together and whispered.

Then they went to King Darius.

'Your Majesty,' they said. 'May you live for ever.

'You are great. You are wonderful. You are like a god.'

'Thank you very much,' said Darius.

'We want you to make a law,' said the men. 'No one may pray to anyone except to you. If anyone disobeys, they will be thrown into a den of lions.'

'What a splendid idea,' said Darius. 'It will be one of my great laws that cannot be changed.'

Daniel always prayed to God.

In the morning.

In the middle of the day.

At the end of the day.

The people he worked with were watching.

The next day, they went to see King Darius.

'Your Majesty,' they said. 'May you live for ever.

'Do you remember the law you made?'

'I do,' said Darius. 'It's a very strict law. If anyone breaks it, I will throw them into a den of lions.'

Then, for a bit of fun, he roared.

'Hooraaaaaah!'

'Your Majesty,' said the men. 'Daniel has broken the law. He keeps on saying prayers to his God.'

Darius stopped making roaring noises. He looked very sad. 'He's not included in the law,' he mumbled.

'Oh, but Your Majesty,' said the men. 'You CANNOT change the law.'

Darius frowned. He fretted. He paced. He pondered.

There was no way out.

'Go on then,' he told his soldiers. 'Go and fetch Daniel. Throw him to the lions.'

As they did so, Darius felt very bad.

'This is all a bit of a mistake,' he called. 'I hope –'

'Excuse me, Your Majesty,' said a soldier, 'please move

along. It's time to block the den shut.'

Darius did not sleep that night. He frowned. He fretted. He paced. He pondered. 'There's no way out for Daniel,' he whimpered. 'No way out at all.'

Down in the pit, Daniel was sitting among the shadows. He couldn't see much in the dark, but he felt sure someone was with him: someone with special power over lions.

First they yawned huge scary yawns. Then they gave little growls and fell asleep.

As soon as it was light, Darius hurried to the pit.

'May Your Majesty live for ever,' said Daniel, cheerfully. 'God sent an angel to save me from the lions.'

'Hoorah!' cried Darius. This time, he didn't roar.

He helped pull Daniel to safety.

'Now,' he said to the soldiers. 'Fetch the men who tried to get rid of Daniel. I think the lions are getting hungry.'

Little Baby Jesus

by Lois Rock
illustrated by Carolyn Cox

Mary goes with Joseph down to Bethlehem.
A crowded inn, a stable room:
an ox makes room for them.

The baby Jesus,
swaddling bands:
but oh! – no baby bed.
Some hay, a blanket:
in a manger
Jesus rests his head.

A flock of sheep
and shepherds,
who watch them
through the night.
An angel with a
message…
more angels
shining bright.

The shepherds go to Bethlehem,
just as the angels say.
They find the baby Jesus,
still sleeping in the hay.

The night-time sky:
some wise men
are following a star.
It lights the road to Bethlehem
where Mary and Jesus are.

Gold, frankincense, a box of myrrh:
these are the gifts they bring
for little baby Jesus
of whom the angels sing.

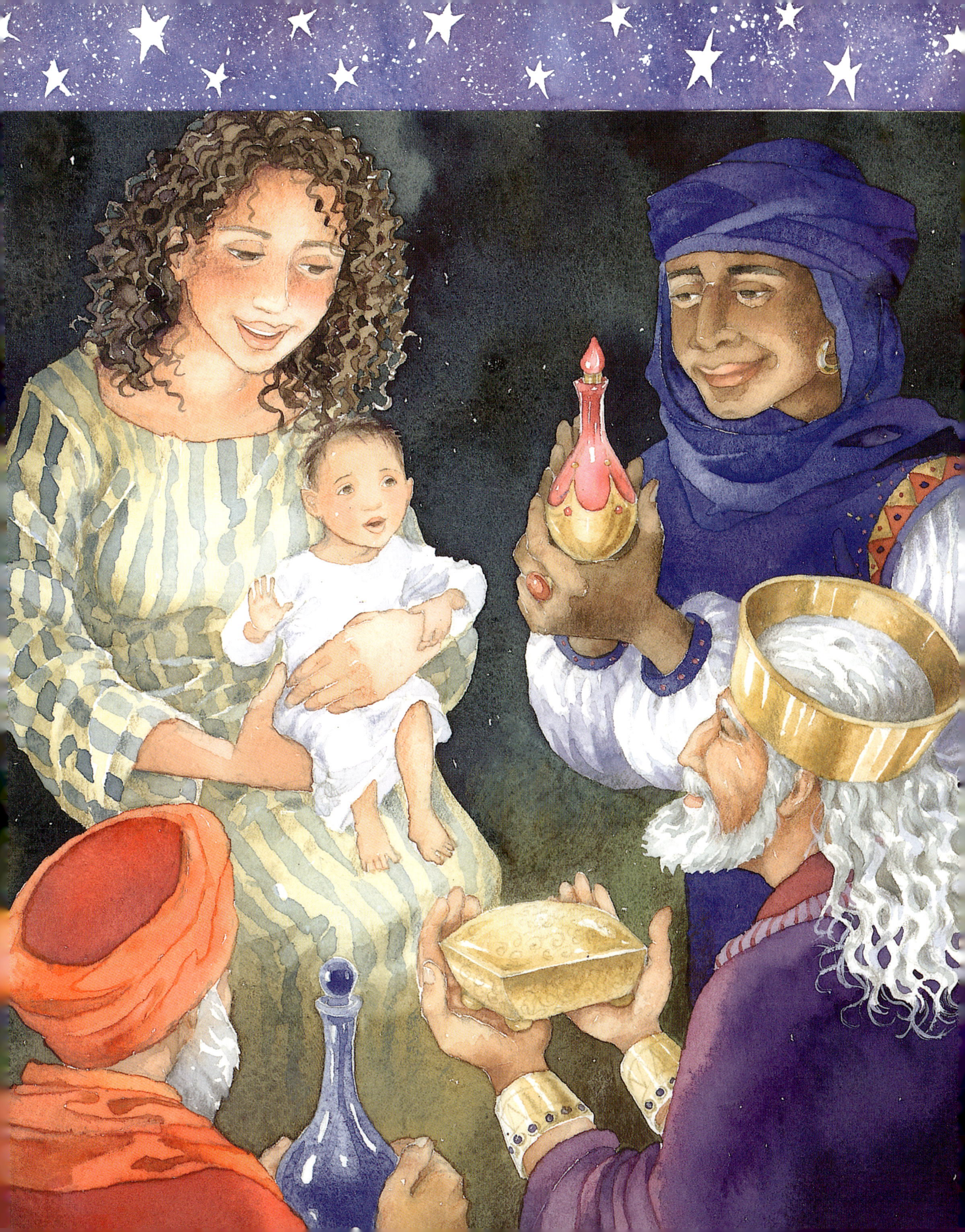

Jesus and the Children

by Sophie Piper
illustrated by Dubravka Kolanovic

When Jesus grew up, he became a preacher. He told people about God and about how much God loves them.

One day, some people brought their children to Jesus. They wanted him to give them his blessing.

Jesus' grown-up friends were cross.

'You mustn't waste Jesus' time,' they said. 'He's so busy preaching. The things he has to say are far too clever and far too important for children.'

Jesus heard what they were saying and he was dismayed.

'Let the children come to me and do not stop them,' he said. 'The kingdom of God belongs to them.'

Looking High and Low for One Lost Sheep

by Christina Goodings ◆ illustrated by Alex Ayliffe

Come closer! A man called Jesus is telling a story. It's about a shepherd who had one hundred sheep. I was one of them.

The shepherd kept us all safe. He led us to the greenest grass. He found pools of clear water for us. And as we played in the sunshine, our shepherd counted us all – from one to a hundred.

At night, when wild animals began to creep from the shadows to go hunting, he called us all into the low-walled fold. As we trotted in, he counted us all, from one to a hundred.

Early one morning I hid so he couldn't see me. But he kept looking and looking till he found me.

So I went a little further to hide. When I heard the shepherd coming, I ran on.

And on.

And on.

I found a clever place to go. The shepherd walked right by. I was all by myself. I had won!

I was all alone as the sun rose higher in the sky.

The shepherd must have walked all morning.

He must have walked at noon, when the sun was hot.

He must have got as far as the lake.

I was all alone as the sun sank low in the afternoon. The shepherd must have walked down to the lake and back again.

I was all alone as the shadows of evening grew long. The shepherd must have gone back to the flock and counted them into the fold for the night. Then I heard a sound.

Oh no!

Could it be a wolf?
Or a fox?

Oh dear!

Or a lion?

Oh help!

It was the shepherd! He smiled and gave a cheer. 'There you are, my little one,' he said.

On the way home he called to his friends. 'I've found my lost sheep. Come and celebrate!'

Jesus came to join in the fun. Now he tells my story over and over again.

Listen to what he's saying. My story has a message for you…

The shepherd is happy to find his sheep. And there is joy in heaven when someone who is lost in life finds the right path.

The Story of the Good Samaritan

by Lois Rock
illustrated by Anthony Lewis

One day, a teacher of the Law came to see Jesus.

'Teacher,' he asked, 'what must I do to gain eternal life?'

'Tell me what our holy books say,' Jesus replied.

'They say, "You must love God with all your heart, with all your soul, with all your strength and with all your mind," and also, "You must love your neighbour as you love yourself."'

'You are right,' said Jesus.

'But who is my neighbour?' asked the teacher.

Jesus told a story.

'There was once a man who was going from Jerusalem to Jericho. Suddenly fierce bandits attacked him. They took all he had and left him for dead.

'Now a priest from the Temple was going that way. He saw the man, but he walked by on the far side of the road.

'Next came a Levite, a helper in the Temple. He saw the man lying in the road and walked over to take a closer look. Then he too hurried on.

'A Samaritan came along. He saw the man and felt sorry for him. He went over to him, cleaned his wounds and put bandages on them. Then he lifted the man onto his donkey and took him to an inn. There, he gave him all the care he needed.

The following day, he gave the innkeeper two silver coins.

'Please take care of this man for me,' he said. 'If it costs more, I will pay the extra when I am here next.'

Jesus turned to the teacher of the Law. 'Well,' he said, 'which of the three was a neighbour to the man in the road?'

'The one who was kind to him,' he replied.

'Then you go and do the same,' said Jesus.

The Great Feast

by Lois Rock
illustrated by Gail Newey

One day, Jesus was a guest at the table of a wealthy man.

Another guest spoke to him: 'How happy are those who will sit down at the feast in the Kingdom of God.'

Jesus replied with a story.

'There was once a man who was giving a great feast. He invited a large number of people. When it was time for the celebration to begin, he sent his servant out with a message for the guests: "Come! The preparations have been made. Everything is ready."

'One by one, they all began to make excuses.

'The first one said, "I have bought a field and must go and look at it. Please tell your master how sorry I am."

'Another said, "I have bought five pairs of oxen and am on my way to try them out; please tell your master how very sorry I am."

'Another one said, "I have just got married. I must spend time with my new family and so I cannot come. Please tell your master how truly sorry I am."

'The servant went back and told his master the news. The man was furious.

'He sent his servant out on a new errand. "Hurry out into the streets and the alleys of the town," he ordered, "and bring back the poor, the crippled, the blind, and the lame."

'The servant swiftly did as he was told, and then returned. "Sir," he said, "your order has been carried out, but there is still room for more."

'So the master said to the servant, "Go out to the country roads and lanes and make people come in. I want my house to be full. But I tell you: those who were first invited but did not come will not taste the dinner."'

Lost and Found

by Pat Alexander
illustrated by Leon Baxter

'Jesus is friends with a lot of bad people. That's not right.' Some people grumbled wherever Jesus went.

'But God loves and cares about *everyone*, not just good people,' Jesus said. And he told them this story…

'Once upon a time, there was a father who had two sons. The older boy helped on the farm. But the younger one said:

'"Give me my share of your money – now. I want to have some fun."

'That made his father sad. But he gave him the money. The boy left home and went far away.

'The fun didn't last: his money was soon spent. The boy got a job. It was feeding the pigs. He was *so* hungry he could have eaten the pig-food!

'He was very unhappy too.

'"This is silly," he thought at last. "Why don't I go home? No one's hungry there. I'll tell Dad I'm sorry I wasted all his money. I don't deserve to be one of the family. But perhaps he'll let me work for him." So he set off for home.

'All this time his father had waited and watched for his boy to come home. Now here he was, coming down the road!

'He ran out to meet him.

'"I'm sorry, Dad. I'm *so* sorry," the boy said. "I don't deserve to be one of the family." But his father just hugged him and kissed him.

'"Fetch the boy some clothes," he shouted. "Dress him up! We're going to have a party! My boy has come home, and I'm so happy! I though I had lost him – but now he is found."

'"Whatever is going on?" the older boy asked, when he came in from work.

'"Your brother has come home, and your father is giving him a party," they told him.

'"A party! After all the trouble he's caused! Dad's never given *me* a party. It's not fair!"

'He wasn't a bit pleased. He was *very* grumpy.

'But his father said to him:

'"You know I love you. I will always love you. One day everything I have will be yours. Please don't sulk. Today is a day to be glad. Your brother has come home, and I'm so happy. I thought I had lost him – but now he is found!"'

The Cross

by Mary Joslin
illustrated by Angelo Ruta

For three years, Jesus travelled up and down the land, preaching and teaching.

He told people about God's love. He told people about God's forgiveness.

He called people to follow him: then, he said, even wrongdoers could change and live good and holy lives.

But there was a problem: some of the leaders of the people did not like Jesus' teaching.

They wanted to get rid of him. They told lies about him. They said he had done wrong things for which he deserved to die.

One sad day, Jesus was crucified.

Even as he hung dying, Jesus said a prayer for the people who had been so cruel.

'Father, forgive them,' he said. 'They don't know what they are doing.'

Jesus died upon the cross:
Day of sadness, day of loss.

Friends, they laid him in a tomb:
Day of weeping, day of gloom.

Sunset faded from the sky:
But God's love can never die.

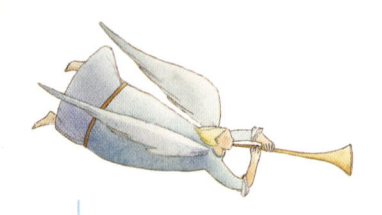

The Easter Angels

by Mary Joslin

illustrated by Elena Temporin

The two women hurried along the path, worried and afraid. In the pale dawn light each bush and tree looked strange and scary.

'Do you think people will recognize us?' asked one. 'Do you think they'll want to capture us, like they captured Jesus? Will they treat us cruelly as well?'

'They might,' whispered the other. Her name was Mary Magdalene and she had been one of Jesus' most loyal friends. She glanced over her shoulder and began to walk even more quickly. 'Even so, they're not going to stop us giving Jesus' body a proper funeral. He was such a good person. He only wanted people to know how much God loves them.'

For a while the two walked on without speaking. They were getting close to the place where Jesus lay in a tomb.

The one who had spoken first had another question:

'How are we going to roll the stone away from the door of the tomb?' she whispered. 'It's too heavy for us, I'm sure.'

Mary Magdalene bit her lip. 'You may be right,' she said. 'I hadn't thought of that.'

All at once their plans for going back to the tomb to wrap Jesus' body with love and care seemed foolish.

'We'll just have to try,' she said, and she sounded very determined. 'Oh no – look! There are Roman soldiers on guard.'

'Now what do we do?' asked the other.

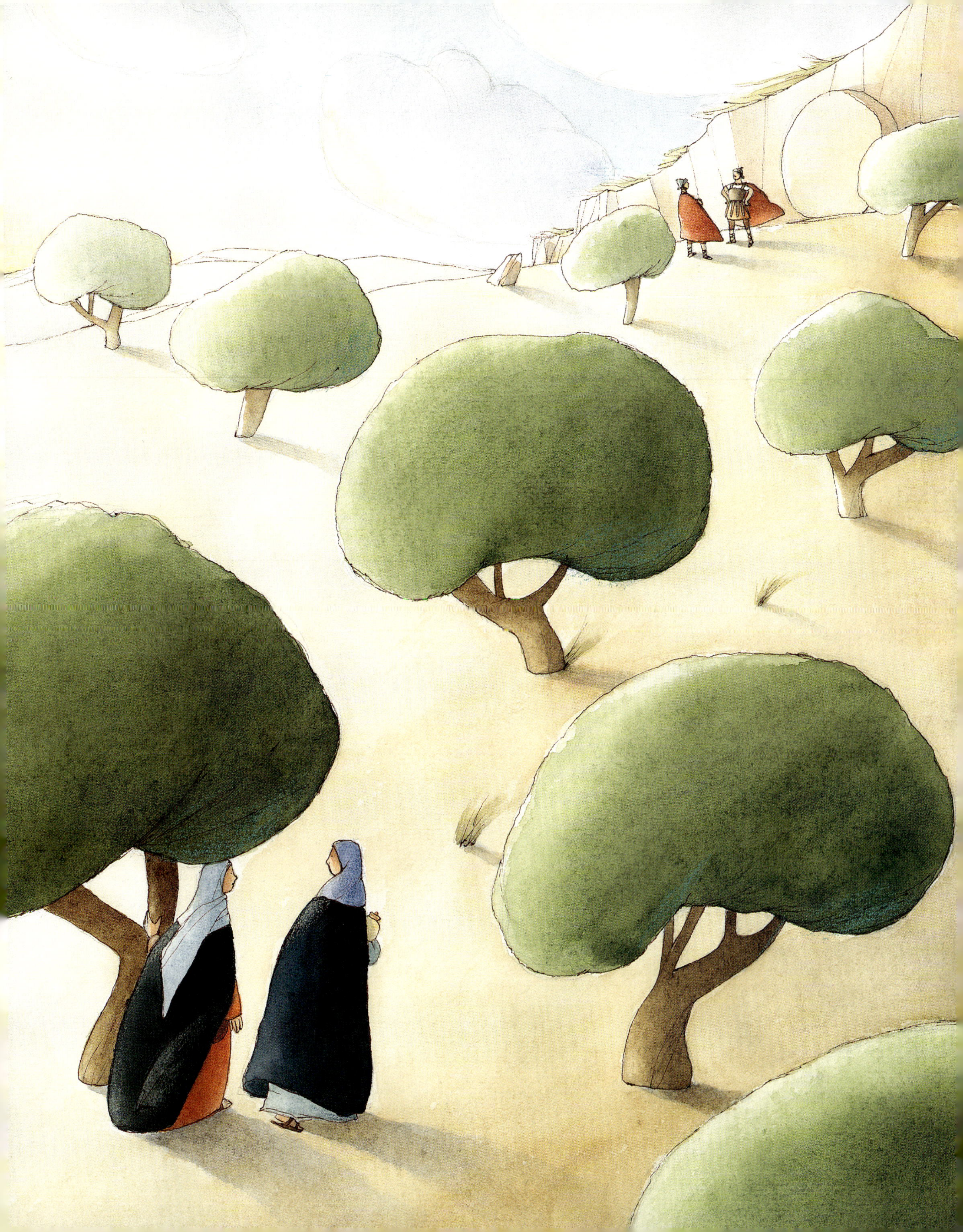

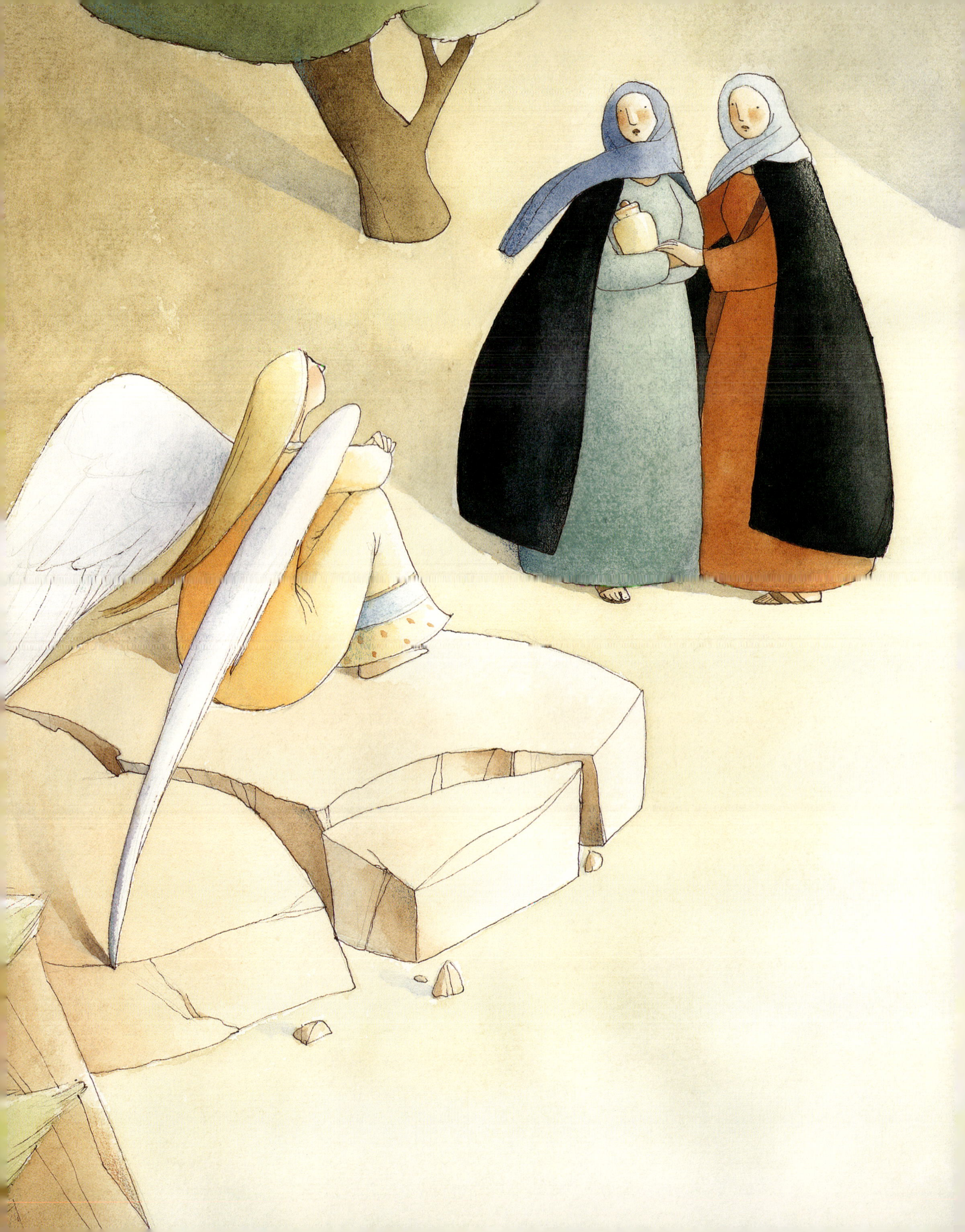

Suddenly there came a low roar like distant thunder: the earth trembled; the trees shook and all the birds sped away, dark shapes in the silver sky.

Lightning flashed down and struck the round stone door to the tomb. In the dazzling light, the women saw the soldiers leap to their feet – and then fall down, stunned and not moving.

The huge door rolled open and fell with a crash. The dust shimmered with light. As it cleared they saw one of God's angels, sitting on the stone.

'Don't be afraid,' said the angel to the women. 'I know you are looking for Jesus, who was crucified. He is not here; God has raised him to life. Look – the place where they laid him is empty.

'Go: tell his friends that their beloved Jesus is going to meet them in Galilee.'

The women turned and ran, full of fear and at the same time thrilled with joy.

All at once, the sky turned gold as the sun floated upwards from beyond the hills. Mary stopped for a moment to gaze in wonder. It seemed as if she was standing at the door of heaven itself.

Compiled by Lois Rock
This edition copyright © 2007 Lion Hudson
Text and illustrations copyright: see acknowledgments below

The moral rights of the authors and illustrators have been asserted

A Lion Children's Book
an imprint of
Lion Hudson plc
Mayfield House, 256 Banbury Road,
Oxford OX2 7DH, England
www.lionhudson.com
ISBN 978 0 7459 6057 9

First edition 2007
10 9 8 7 6 5 4 3 2 1 0

All rights reserved

A catalogue record for this book is available from the British Library

Typeset in Baskerville MT Schoolbook
Printed and bound in China

Acknowledgments
Cover (clockwise from top left): Estelle Corke, Susie Poole, Ruth Rivers, Richard Johnson, Alex Ayliffe, Kristina Stephenson, Anthony Lewis. Copyright © Individual illustrators listed above.

Endpapers: 'Quietly in the Morning' by Lois Rock, first published in *The Lion Book of 1000 Prayers for Children*. Text copyright © 2003 Lion Hudson. 'In the Easter Garden' by Lois Rock, first published in *The Lion Book of 1000 Prayers for Children*. Copyright © 2003 Lion Hudson. Illustrations from *My Baptism Book*. Illustrations copyright © 2006 Dubravka Kolanovic.

In the Beginning: Adapted from *My Very First Bible*. Text copyright © 2003 Lion Hudson. Illustrations copyright © 2003 Alex Ayliffe.

The First Rainbow: Adapted from *The First Rainbow*. Text copyright © 2000 Lion Hudson. Illustrations copyright © 2000 Susie Poole.

Baby Moses, Brave Moses: Adapted from text from *The Lion Book of Five-Minute Bible Stories*. Text copyright © 2004 Lion Hudson. Illustrations copyright © 2004 Richard Johnson.

David and His Song: First published in *The Lord is My Shepherd*. Text copyright © 2004 Lion Hudson. Illustrations copyright © 2004 Ruth Rivers.

Jonah and the Big Fish: Adapted from text from *The Baby Bible*. Text copyright © 2006 Sarah Toulmin. Illustration copyright © 2006 Kristina Stephenson.

Daniel and the Lions: First published in *Bible Story Time. Daniel and the Lions*. Text copyright © 2005 Lion Hudson. Illustrations copyright © 2005 Estelle Corke.

Little Baby Jesus: First published in *Let's Read the Christmas Story*. Copyright © 2004 Lion Hudson. Illustrations from *My Book of Christmas*. Illustrations copyright © 2005 Carolyn Cox.

Jesus and the Children: First published in *My Baptism Book*. Text copyright © 2006 Lion Hudson. Illustrations copyright © 2006 Dubravka Kolanovic.

Looking High and Low for One Lost Sheep: Adapted text copyright © 2000 Lion Hudson. Illustrations copyright © 2000 Alex Ayliffe.

The Story of the Good Samaritan: First published in *A Child's First Story of Jesus*. Text copyright © 2004 Lion Hudson. Illustrations copyright © 2004 Anthony Lewis.

The Great Feast: First published in *Best-Loved Parables*. Text copyright © 1998 Lion Hudson. Illustrations copyright © 1998 Gail Newey.

The Loving Father: Adapted from *The Lion First Bible*. Text copyright © 1997 Pat Alexander. Illustrations copyright © 1997 Leon Baxter.

The Cross: First published in *Best-Loved Prayers*. Text copyright © 2006 Lion Hudson. Illustrations copyright © 2006 Angelo Ruta.

The Easter Angels: First published in *The Lion Treasury of Angel Stories*. Text copyright © 2006 Lion Hudson. Illustrations copyright © 2006 Elena Temporin.